DISCUSSION PAPER 72

I0026772

INEQUALITY AND IDENTITY
Causes of War?

GÖRAN HOLMQVIST

NORDISKA AFRIKAINSTITUTET, UPPSALA 2012

Indexing terms:
Africa
Civil war
Conflicts
Social inequality
Cultural identity
Intergroup relations
Social control
Theory
Comparative analysis

Language checking: Peter Colenbrander

ISSN 1104-8417

ISBN 978-91-7106-714-2

© The author and Nordiska Afrikainstitutet 2011

Production: Byrå4

Print on demand, Lightning Source UK Ltd.

Contents

Abstract

Four theories on the causes of civil war are reviewed. One theory, identified with Paul Collier, emphasises feasibility factors over factors related to grievance; a second theory, identified with Frances Stewart, is built around the role of horizontal inequalities; a third theory, identified with William Zartman, highlights the different roles "need, creed and greed" factors play in various phases of a conflict; and a fourth theory, identified with the World Bank/World Development Report 2011, points out as a crucial factor "commitment" problems leading to institutional failures. The four theories lead to quite different policy conclusions. Their strengths and weaknesses, and their claimed empirical support, are discussed.

The second part of the paper presents empirical explorations, based on Afrobarometer data, to shed additional light on some of the mechanisms that underpin these theories: how horizontal inequalities between ethnic groups are linked to grievances; how horizontal inequalities compare with vertical inequalities as a correlate of conflict indicators and how some of the elaborated indicators have evolved over time in the case of a recent violent conflict (Kenya). No claims on directions of causality are made, but results do indicate that horizontal inequalities, in different dimensions, are important factors in grievances and violent conflicts. Future research directions are identified.

Introduction

During the Cold War era, conflicts often presented themselves, at least at the rhetorical level, as about ideology and class, following the East/West division. After the Cold War, a growing share of conflicts have been classified as "ethnic conflicts" (60 per cent in 2005 as against approximately 30 per cent in the 1960s (Stewart 2008, p. 6)). Whether this reflects a fundamental change in the character of the conflicts, or whether, rather, the Cold War concealed the true nature of many conflicts, is a subject of some debate (Arnson and Zartman 2005, p. 2). In any event, the fact that so many severe and long-lasting civil wars persisted after the Cold War and could no longer be understood in terms of its geopolitical logic did inspire renewed academic debate about the causes of civil war. Factors related to economics and identity were given a more prominent role in this research agenda.

Inequality and identity as causes of civil war are the subject of this paper. Part 1 provides a review of the way in which identity and inequality have been dealt with in four contributions that represent different strands of the post-Cold War literature on the causes of civil war. Each of them has presented a "story" – theories combined with empirical evidence – on the causes of civil war and the role played by identity and inequality. To keep it simple, we label them the "Collier story", the "Stewart story", the "Zartman story" and the "Commitment story."[1] In essence, the Paul Collier story is one about civil war occurring when it is financially and militarily feasible, while downplaying the role of objective social grievances. The Frances Stewart story is one about horizontal inequalities between identity groups being a main driver of conflict. The William Zartman story is one about a stylised sequencing of civil war, with different factors being decisive in different phases (greed factors of military entrepreneurs likely to become dominant over time). The Commitment story emphasises a lack of trust and failing institutions as an obstacle to agreement among conflicting parties on non-violent solutions. These four stories also lead to quite different policy conclusions. Promoting a healthy economy and transparency of trade in extractive resources are some of the policy conclusions following from the Collier story. Affirmative actions against horizontal inequality in its various manifestations become a key recommendation in the Stewart story. The importance of identifying the right moment for external actors to intervene in civil wars – not too late, when greed-related interests in perpetuating the conflict have built up – is one important message from Zartman. The importance of investing in appropriate

---

1.   Four books giving an overview of these stories are Collier and Sambinis (2005), Stewart (2008), Arnson and Zartman (2005) and World Bank (2011).

institutional frameworks and citizens' trust is a prominent policy conclusion in the World Development Report 2011.

Part 2 of this paper presents some preliminary empirical results based on Afrobarometer data, which is an opinion survey carried out repeatedly in some 20 sub-Saharan African countries. This part is an exploratory attempt to shed additional light on some of the assumptions and mechanisms underpinning these four theories, based on indicators elaborated from survey data on identity groups, group grievances and inequalities.

On the concepts of inequality and identity

To start, just a few words on some distinctions between inequality and identity. Both are tricky concepts and could be the subject of lengthy discussion. In the context of this paper, we may limit ourselves to the following distinctions.

When it comes to inequality, there is an *"inequality between what"* question that may have different answers. What is often labelled "vertical inequality" relates to differences between individuals in a given population, while "horizontal inequality" refers to differences between the averages within different groups. There is also an *"inequality in what"* question, for instance, in incomes, assets, political influence, social services, cultural status, etc. Finally there is an *"inequality – how measured"* question, with a number of possible ways of mathematically transforming an array of numbers into a single indicator reflecting how "unequal" these numbers are (GINI indexes, polarisation indexes, Theil indexes, etc.).

All of us carry different identities. They may be more or less enduring and more or less important to the holder and to others. For the analysis of civil wars, it has mainly been identities related to ethnicity, class, religion and region that have attracted interest. In conceptualising identity, it is common to distinguish between *"primordial"*, *"instrumentalist"* and *"social constructivist"* notions of identity (Brown and Langer 2010). The primordial notion, that identities somehow are essentialist or given by nature, is frequently criticised. However, it is hard to find any social scientist who really is a proponent of a primordial notion of identity. The anthropologist Clifford Geertz's contributions from the 1960s are sometimes associated with a primordial position, but in fact he did not claim that identities (linked to such aspects as common blood or kinship) were "primordial," but rather that what distinguishes them is that they are "are seen" to be primordial, which is a different proposition (see Brown and Langer 2010 for a more thorough discussion).

Most social scientists would probably agree with the instrumentalist notion in the sense that they accept the idea that identities are sometimes exploited as tools for political mobilisation or political domination. Most social scientist would probably also agree that an individual may carry various identities and that these identities are fluid and constructed as a result of social processes. However, when it comes to more concrete strategies to study identities, there are large differences between social scientists over how much importance to place on the fluidity, constructedness, plurality and instrumentality of identities. At the one end, one finds econometric studies using ethno-religious categories as an independent variable, using categories given, for instance, by the Soviet atlas of languages and religions, which was established in the 1960s: in other words, this is an empirical strategy open to criticism for taking identities as permanent, exhaustive and exclusive. At the other end of the spectrum, one finds proponents of the idea of studying "identities without groups" or "identification processes," rather than identity groups (Brubaker 2002), or who propose discourse analysis as an alternative to more traditional empirical approaches "to capture the cluster of relationships within which identities have meaning and trace changes in them over time" (Fierke 2007).

PART 1
Four stories on inequality and identity as causes of civil war

The Collier Story

In the so-called "greed vs. grievance" debate, Paul Collier is probably the most influential exponent of an "economics of war" approach, which emphasises factors related to opportunity for and feasibility of financing and organising rebellions as determinants of the risk of civil war, as against factors related to objective grievances. There are a number of both older and more recent contributions with similar or related messages (Grossman 1991; Hirschleifer 2001; Fearon and Laitin 2003: see Kalyvas 2007 for an overview). The so called Collier-Hoeffler model was first presented in 1998 (Collier and Hoeffler 1998) and then followed by a number of subsequent contributions (Collier and Hoeffler 2002; Collier and Hoeffler 2004; Collier, Hoeffler and Söderbom 2004; Collier and Hoeffler 2008). Empirical results and interpretations are not entirely consistent between these contributions. The (to my knowledge) most recent publication – *Beyond Greed and Grievance: Feasibility and Civil War* (2008) – reviews and revises empirical findings and nuances interpretations of results and the main messages. In fairness to the authors, this latest publication is the one referred to below as the "Collier story" (unless otherwise indicated).

The key hypothesis of the Collier story has been formulated as follows (Collier and Hoeffler 2008):

• Factors that are important for the financial and military feasibility of rebellion, but are unimportant for motivation, decisively increase the risk of civil war.

"Feasiblity" refers to factors that facilitate, financially and militarily, the organisation of a large-scale rebellion. "Motivations" are of two kinds: "greed" and "grievances." According to Collier, "the feasibility hypothesis proposes that where rebellion is feasible it will occur." Motivation as "grievance" (let us think of it as discontent in a certain identity group), on the other hand, is indeterminate and is always around to be exploited. The fact that grievances often are part of the discourse in a rebellion does not mean that they are a factor that explains why conflicts happen in some countries but not in others. Also greed (we may think of it as rebels motivated by the prospect of illegal income) may be seen as endogenous in relation to the outbreak of a civil war, stimulated by the opportunities that are opened up by a conflict, but not as a main factor explaining why conflicts occur in some countries and not in others.

The empirical test to verify these hypothesis are regression analyses (logit regressions) estimating which factors contribute to the risk of the outbreak of a civil war. Some case-study support is also provided in Collier and Sambinis (2005), where econometric findings are combined with country studies that were designed to shed additional light on the predictive strength of the Collier and Hoeffler model. The regression analysis is based on a database with over 1,000 observations (countries/years). The variables that are reported as significant in the various model specifications, and as core results, are (direction of impact on the risk of civil war in parenthesis):

- level of GDP/capita, also remaining robust for some tests of reverse causality (−)
- growth of GDP per capita (−)
- primary commodity exports as share of GDP (+)
- peace duration, number of years since last civil war (−)
- population size (+)
- social fractionalisation, i.e., probability that two randomly chosen persons are not of the same language, combined with a similar measure for religion (+)

Also, being a former French colony in Africa between 1965 and 1999, when a French security umbrella was provided, appears to have reduced the risk of civil war (by making rebellion more costly, is the interpretation). "Proportion young men" and "mountainous terrain" have the expected positive significance in accordance with the feasibility hypothesis, but are not significant in most model specifications.

Something that casts doubt on these "core results," and which is not highlighted by Collier and Hoeffler (2008), is that the significance of the GDP per capita variable and the social fractionalisation variable does not survive the inclusion of a dummy variable for sub-Saharan Africa. The fact that Africa is unusually affected by wars, has low GDP per capita and is relatively fractionalised apparently drives some of these "core results" to an extent. However, a dummy for sub-Saharan Africa could be a proxy for so many things, opening up a range of interpretation beyond GDP and fractionalisation, and casts some doubt on the robustness of the core results.

The most critical aspect of the Collier story is the interpretation of these empirical results as supporting the "feasibility hypothesis." As recognised in Collier and Hoeffler (2008), the results may, in fact, lend themselves to various alternative interpretations supporting different hypotheses. For instance, the favoured interpretation of the GDP variables is that a low level of GDP, or low GDP growth, is related to lower costs of recruiting rebels (low GDP/low growth means lower salaries/fewer jobs) or possibly as something related to the ability of the state to deter rebellion. However, having low growth or lagging behind neighbouring countries in terms of GDP per capita may also relate to grievances, which would go against the feasibility hypothesis. Similarly, the favoured interpretation of the natural resource variable is that it increases the feasibility of financing rebellion. Alternative interpretations, not consistent with the feasibility hypothesis, are that the existence of natural resources may motivate rebels to capture rents ("greed") or be linked to governance problems ("natural resource curse," uneven development producing losers and winners, etc.), which would, hence, be an interpretation in terms of grievances. Of the three variables that are claimed to more unambiguously support the feasibility hypothesis – "mountainous terrain," "French security umbrella" and "proportion of young men" – only "French security umbrella" seems to produce reasonably consistent and significant results.

When it comes to identity and inequality, the main point of interest in the present paper, Collier and Hoeffler (2008) point out "social fractionalisation" as a factor that significantly increases the risk of civil war, while they report that "none of the measures of inequality were significant."

Their social fractionalisation variable measures the probability that two randomly chosen individuals of a population do not speak the same language, and combines it with a similar measure for religion. This data, taken from Fearon and Latin (2003), who in turn compiled their data from the Soviet *Atlas Norodav Mira* (1964) in combination with data from the CIA Factbook. Data on linguistic and religious identity groups are thus taken as given by history and unchanging over time and are treated as an exogenous variable in the regressions. This is an empirical strategy that might open the way for criticism on the grounds of being "primordial." However, the Collier story's concept of identity is probably more accurately described as "instrumentalist": identity markers are always around but become salient when entrepreneurs of violence are given an opportunity to exploit them. A weakness of this fractionalisation index, which is also recognised in Collier and Sabinis (2005, p. 319), is that it is a very crude measure if what we are concerned about is politically relevant fractionalisation.

The inequality measures used in Collier and Hoeffler (2008) are not spelled out, but in previous studies the vertical GINI over incomes and land ownership was used. This does not capture inequality between groups. The missing data are a problem when it comes to inequality measures, seriously affecting the sample size when introduced into the regressions.

Unlike Collier and Hoeffler (2008), some previous Collier studies have presented results going in other directions in relation to identity and inequality. In Collier and Hoeffler (2004), both ethnic and religious fractionalisation were in fact reported as something that made a society safer from civil war, as long as "ethnic dominance" (one ethnic group having a 45 to 90 per cent share of population) was avoided. On income inequality, Collier, Hoeffler and Söderbom (2004) reported it as a significant factor (in a study explaining the *duration* of civil wars, hence not the same independent variable as the other studies).

The differences among empirical results over the years are not particularly surprising, given that the database used has expanded and new model specifications have evolved. However, of interest here are the divergent interpretations that have been placed upon these results. When social fractionalisation was found to reduce the risk of civil war in Collier and Hoeffler (2004), the interpretation was one supporting the feasibility hypothesis: both high fractionalisation and no fractionalisation at all make a society safer because rebel organisations have more difficulty in maintaining cohesion when they need to span different social groups. This interpretation is absent in Collier and Hoeffler (2008), where social fractionalisation is found to increase the risk of war significantly. Similarly, when inequality was not found to be significant in Collier and Hoeffler (2004), inequality was interpreted as a proxy for grievance and its insignificance hence interpreted as supporting the feasibility hypothesis. But when income inequality was found to be a significant factor in the duration of civil wars (Collier, Hoeffler and Söderbom 2004) there was an opening for an alternative interpretation compatible with the feasibility hypothesis: inequality could be a proxy for the cost of recruitment, "since recruits tend to come from the poor, for a given mean per capita income, the greater is inequality the lower will be recruitment cost."

To summarise, the Collier story on identity and inequality is far from crystal clear: econometric results have been pointing in different directions over the years and there seems to be an element of opportunism in the way these results have been interpreted to support the feasibility hypothesis. Furthermore, the indicators used that are supposed to reflect "grievance" are far from ideal if the purpose is to test the feasibility hypothesis against alternatives affording a stronger role to causes related to motivations.

The Stewart Story

Conflict between different identity groups (ethnic, religious, regional) is a salient feature of many civil wars. However, most multiethnic or multi-religious societies are peaceful. The critical question that guides Stewart is why violent conflicts between different identity groups break out in some circumstances and not in others. The heart of the Stewart story is that group identities tend to lead to violent conflicts when they overlap with inequalities. Inequalities between groups are labelled "horizontal inequalities" and may have different dimensions: economic horizontal inequalities refer to differences in access to assets, incomes and employment opportunities; social horizontal inequalities refer to differences in access to social services; political horizontal inequalities to differences in political opportunities and power; and cultural horizontal inequalities to differences in recognition and standing of language, religion and customs. These inequalities may be captured by different measures, reviewed in Stewart (2008), with the group GINI (or horizontal as opposed to vertical GINI) being preferred, although alternative measures may have some advantages depending on purpose.

The concept of identity in the Stewart story is claimed to follow a social constructivist line, recognising that group identities may be shaped and mobilised as a result of conflicts. However, it is also argued "that people themselves can be strongly convinced about the essential nature of their identities and that of others – which is why mobilization by identity can work" (Stewart 2008, p. 10). Identity may thus be a dependent variable at one point in history, but can act as an independent variable in a later context. Identities viewed as "constructed but sticky" are thus a core ingredient in the Stewart story.

In Stewart (2008) four hypotheses are formulated (pp. 18–19):
- Conflict is more likely where there are significant political or economic horizontal inequalities, or both.
- Political mobilisation is especially likely where there are consistent horizontal inequalities (political and economic horizontal inequalities run in the same direction).
- Lack of cultural recognition and equity, or cultural status horizontal inequalities, will be provocative, while cultural inclusion will help sustain peace.
- Political mobilisation and possibly conflict is more likely where horizontal inequalities are widening.

The Stewart story does not, however, exclude the influence of factors other than horizontal inequalities. Economic factors such as low GDP, low growth and natural resource dependency may influence the likelihood of civil wars through various mechanisms, some of which may be related to widening horizontal inequalities and others to facilitating the financing of a rebellion.

There are three kinds of empirical evidence presented in support of these hypotheses: i) quantitative studies based on cross-country data, ii) quantitative intra-country studies based on district-level data, and iii) qualitative case-study evidence.

Data limitations are obviously a constraint in providing econometric evidence, as data on horizontal inequalities are not readily available. Östby (2008) uses data from demographic health surveys (55 countries, 1986-2003) to calculate economic and social horizontal inequalities between ethnic, religious and regional groups, based on indicators of household assets and average years of education. Her study reveals a significant rise in the probability of conflict in countries with severe horizontal inequalities. Cederman *et al.* (2010) use a data set on spatial distribution of economic activity within countries (G-Econ dataset, 1991–2005) to show that both those groups that are either affluent or poor relative to the national average are more likely to engage in conflict. Similar findings are presented in Brown (2010). There are also examples of quantitative intra-country studies which indicate that the likelihood or intensity of conflict is greater where horizontal inequalities are more pronounced (Indonesia treated in Mancini (2008) and Nepal in Murshed and Gates (2005)). Qualitative case studies supporting elements of the Stewart story are numerous (Ghana, Côte d'Ivoire, Nigeria, Bolivia, Guatemala, Peru, Southeast Asia, see Stewart (2008)).

We limit ourselves to pointing out two critical aspects in the Stewart story.

The first concerns the link from externally measured horizontal inequalities to perceived horizontal inequalities. The Stewart story is one about people taking actions on the basis of perceptions of others and of their relative position, rather than on the basis of actual inequality. The measures of horizontal inequality in the studies cited above do, however, use externally measured horizontal inequalities without capturing what the perceptions are among the groups concerned. Stewart (2008) contains some studies (Ghana and Nigeria) that have tried to establish the link between actual inequalities and perceived inequalities, but the results are not entirely consistent and reveal some puzzling paradoxes (Langer and Ukiwo 2008). "To what extent people's perceptions of horizontal inequality accurately reflect a country's objective political and economic reality is an important empirical question," according to Brown and Langer (2010). (In Part 2 below this empirical question will be approached again.)

A second critical aspect of the Stewart story has to do with causal directions. How misleading is it to treat horizontal inequalities as an independent variable in relation to conflicts when it is known that both identities and inequalities may be shaped and strengthened as a result of conflicts? This problem of endogeneity is there even if horizontal inequalities are measured well ahead of the onset of a civil war, as these horizontal inequalities may be the result of previous conflicts or tendencies towards conflict (which may have laid the foundations for the civil war). One line of defence could be that horizontal inequalities remain relatively stable over time, and in some cases where data are available, this seems to be the case (Östby 2008, p. 145). In Stewart and Langer (2008) a long list of factors that tend to explain this persistence is reviewed. However, there are also indications that violent conflicts have considerably effects on inequalities: a review based on cross-country panel data for 1960-2005 indicates clearly rising levels of vertical inequality (up two points) during war and early postwar reconstruction (Bircan, Bruck and Vothknecht 2010). Furthermore, not only may inequalities be related to previous conflicts but, as pointed out by many scholars (Brown and Langer 2010), identities themselves may be shaped by inequalities, becoming less pronounced as inequality is reduced, and vice versa. There are hence a multitude of potential causal pathways to be mapped by a limited number of data points.

The Zartman Story

Whether conflicts are about resources, identity or basic needs is a question of no interest in the Zartman story, which accepts that all conflicts contain these elements of "need, creed and greed." The interesting question is rather how these factors relate to each other in causing and sustaining conflict, and how, not whether, conflict is related to these factors. Unlike Collier's and Stewart's stories, the Zartman story does not build its case on econometric results from large cross-country studies. "Such studies do not explain civil conflict, they explain conflict with more than 1,000 deaths, which is a bit like explaining human growth by starting at the age of 12 years" (Zartman 2005, p. 262). The Zartman story is, rather, built on in-depth case studies to test explanatory propositions based on data that tend to be longitudinal or sequential. It aims at establishing a model of the process of generating and sustaining violent conflict that is supported by enough significant cases to be testworthy, which as a next step can subjected to more refined analysis. The Zartman story is hence a stylised and idealised version of civil wars and does not claim to provide a scale replication of reality faithful in all its details.

This stylised Zartman model of civil war would contain the following sequences:

- "The need phase": A weakened or collapsed state is the starting point. A weakened state becomes unable to address the needs of its citizens, of the majority of them or of certain segments. Grievances build up (could be poverty, inequalities, discrimination, injustices, etc.).
- "The creed phase": Political entrepreneurs are activated and will exploit these grievances by seizing on some preexisting identity factor as a convenient handle to mobilise support. It could be ethnicity or some other identity. "Creed" hence becomes an element in the conflict.
- "The greed phase": Conflict may end in asymmetrical victory or in some kind of settlement. But when conflicts do not follow this "natural course" and become prolonged and bogged-down, then the greed factor sets in "as the temptation to turn the means into ends begins to rise."

The examples mentioned of conflicts that have outright state collapse at their roots are Sierra Leone and Angola. Other cases that have begun with a lesser degree of state failure are Lebanon, Colombia and Afghanistan. In all the cases reviewed, when the opportunity arose on the basis of felt need, political entrepreneurs seized on some identity factor to mobilise support. UNITA in Angola exploited ethnic identities, FARC in Colombia exploited geography and class while in Afghanistan the Taliban primarily exploited a nontribal religious identity. Prolonged conflicts where the greed factor (related to drugs, diamonds and other forms of natural-resource extraction) became strong are those in Colombia, Afghanistan, Angola, Congo and Sierra Leone (Zartman 2005, p. 273).

The policy conclusions that follow from this model are quite straightforward. In the first phase, prevention of conflict depends above all on strengthening the state so as to enable it to address the needs of its citizens. In the second phase, the creed phase, control of conflict requires first of all suspension of violence and then the crafting of a new political solution capable of responding to the grievances that caused the conflict in the first place. Finally, the daunting difficulties in dealing with violent conflicts bogged down in the greed phase underscore the importance of addressing conflicts before they reach that stage. Once they have, the only way to bring "greedy leaders" under control is to threaten or eliminate the supply of money and power, which is difficult to do without military force.

Commitment stories

The World Development Report 2011 has conflict, security and development as its theme. It presents a broad overview of research findings and is best characterised as eclectic in its approach. However, if one theoretical current dominates the report it is the emphasis on commitment problems. When parties have opposing interests, and there is a lack of trust and lack of institutions, then this will result in their failing to agree credibly to abstain from violence. This is also clearly reflected in the report's policy recommendations, which emphasise the role of citizen confidence and credible institutions.

It is recognised in the report (p. 76) that a major source of inspiration for this theoretical framework has been the contribution by Nobel laureate Douglas North in his *Violence and Social Orders* (North, Wallis and Weingast 2009). This is an influential book, with the humble sub-title *A Conceptual Framework for Interpreting Recorded Human History*. Its starting point is that violence is the fundamental problem any social order has to resolve. This is one of the most basic reasons why we have states, but making "the deal" which involves the control of this state carries with it a fundamental commitment problem: how can anyone be trusted to stick to a deal if given unconstrained power? The normal way this is solved, labelled the "Natural State" or "limited access regime" in Douglas North's framework, is through a coalition of elites who provide protection to subordinates in return for various forms of privilege. Through checks, balances and personal relations, the elites are able to overcome their internal commitment problems. Only gradually may such Natural States evolve into "open access regimes," that is liberal regimes with political and economic pluralism (only 23 states have made such a transition according to North, a transition to be seen as exceptional and difficult and not as a teleological endpoint). To make the transition, a state needs to go through some critical "doorstep condition": i) rule of law for the elites; ii) the creation of impersonal, perpetually lived organisations in private and public spheres (state institutions and private companies); and iii) consolidated control of the military. Overcoming the commitment problems that are obstacles to the formation of institutions that may control violence is hence a key factor in this model. It is also a model that emphasises the role of elites in gradually establishing these institutions, first among themselves and then, step by step, encompassing increasingly large segments of society.

Commitment problems may, however, come in many forms. Another "grand story" (apparently less influential in the World Development Report 2011), which, just as Douglas North does, emphasises credible commitments and institutions, is Acemoglu and Robinson's *Economic Origins of Dictatorship and Democracy* (2006). In this model, the assumption is that democratisation develops as an elite response to claims for redistribution by "the people." In periods when the masses are unusually mobilised, these claims become threatening to the elite. The elite then seek a deal – redistribution for law and order – but is unable to strike such a deal because its monopoly on power enables it to turn away from its promises in the future when the masses are less mobilised. The solution then becomes building institutions, that is, democracy, which makes it possible for the elite to commit with credibility. In contrast to Douglas North's framework, where the institutions somehow are formed by elites and then gradually envelop society, here the demands by social forces working from below play a decisive role. Interestingly for the topic of this paper, Acemoglu's formal modelling explicitly includes income inequality as a variable, and identifies it as an important obstacle (in some contexts[2]) to the formation of democratic institutions. The intuition behind this result is that institutions involving one-man, one-vote become more threatening to elites the more the advantages and privileges they possess in relation to the masses – democratic institutions then risk becoming too costly for them as a commitment device.

It could be argued that Acemoglu's story – with the masses on the barricades – has little to do with political realities in many fragile developing countries today. However, the basic driving forces of the model may have wider applications: institutions are formed under pressure, as leaps, when unusual events occur, and the "deals" these institutions are built on may require some form of reciprocity (such as one-man one-vote). For the privileged, such reciprocity might be threatening: for the unprivileged, the distrust of powerful adversaries makes demobilisation appear riskier. Hence, the link to inequality.

Another Nobel laureate who has made contributions related to the themes discussed here is Akerlof, with his *Identity Economics*. His starting point is the

---

2.   Very low levels of inequality could also make the move towards democracy less likely. Acemoglu's real world example for this would be Singapore.

assumptions that "belongingness" –having an identity shared with others – is a basic human drive. We like to do things that somehow confirm such identities. Akerlof explicitly includes these considerations in the kind of utility functions economists use to model human behaviour. Certain actions are such that they confirm one's identity and we derive utility from them, just as we get something out of consuming apples and butter. Akerlof's contribution that is of interest here is the notion that identities may be cooperative as well as non-cooperative (Akerlof and Kranton 2000). We may think of them as positive or negative externalities originating from actions we undertake to confirm our identity on the utility of other identity holders. An example of a positive spill-over effect, of cooperative identities, would be: "My actions that serve to uphold my identity as a 'good teacher' are boosted by your actions to uphold your identity as a 'good student', and vice versa." But you can think of the opposite as well: If to assume the identity of "'a respectable Englishmen' you should wear a tie and speak with an Eton accent," then the tie and the accent are identity markers that may exclude some from being "respectable Englishmen." The social function of a tie here is that wearing it is uncomfortable for someone doing manual work, and the function of the accent is to exclude those who have not attended certain (expensive) schools. Those who feel excluded by such identity markers may adopt countervailing strategies – wearing trousers that reveal half their underwear is Akerlof's example – that offend "respectable citizens," who may be unaware of how their identity markers have offended and excluded others in the first place. Identities may thus create positive as well as negative external effects on other identities, which sometimes may be cooperative or neutral, and sometimes highly non-cooperative. Akerlof does not really explain why we end up in one or the other identity, but it does not take much imagination to speculate about the role of inequality as one factor. Unequal access to resources may make it easier to create identity markers that are exclusionary ("ties and Eton accents"), which in turn may prompt counter-reactions in terms of other non-cooperative identity markers. The forming of cooperative identities could hence be understood as a delicate collective choice – hence a commitment problem once again, with inequality as a potential source.

How do these "grand stories," with their emphasis on obstacles to credible commitments, relate to our previous stories? In a way they may be seen as reinforcing some aspects of the Stewart and Zartman stories, as commitment problems could be something that is placed on the causal pathway from inequality to violence, if interpreted along the lines of Acemoglu and Akerlof. Unequal access to resources may obstruct deals that require reciprocity and mutual commitments. And unequal access to resources may be used to establish exclusionary identity markers. But such commitment models also suggest a different mechanism from models that emphasise grievances. Horizontal inequalities, as in the

Stewart story, are primarily a source of grievances, but horizontal inequalities could also be a source of institutional failure, for instance, identity groups being unable to make credible commitments in deals to avoid violence. Both Akerlof and Acemoglu point out some potential mechanisms at play. But "distrust" (horizontal as well as vertical), rather than grievances, then becomes a key variable of interest. This also points to the possibility that in order to build trust and institutions, you may need to address inequalities, a perspective less prominent in the policy recommendations of the World Development Report.

Further complexities and nuances

The Zartman story took a first step in complicating an oversimplified greed vs. grievance – or feasibility vs. motivation – debate by pointing out that all these factors must be part of the understanding of the dynamics of a conflict. A somewhat similar questioning of the greed vs. grievance distinction, complicating things even further, is found in Kalyvas (2003). His point is, however, not that these factors have distinctive roles in different phases of a conflict, but rather that they tend to operate simultaneously at the different levels of a conflict among the local and central actors: the farther you move down to the local level, the more you see of local settling of old scores and of private motivation. Hence, civil wars must often be understood in terms of "alliances" among actors with distinct identities and motivations at local and central levels. An additional layer of complexity is reached in moving down to the level of the individual, and in recognising that several, not necessarily consistent, identities may coexist, making attempts to establish boundaries and to categorise difficult or even questionable.

How would the tellers of the "grand stories" react to such criticism? Probably none of them would deny the existence of any of these complications and nuances. They would all be open to the role of entrepreneurs in exploiting identities, to greed factors evolving over time and to the fact that the key actors in a conflict must often be understood as coalitions among highly divergent interests. But they would probably claim that they attempt to explain why conflicts become more violent and more enduring in some cases than in others. It is the common pattern, rather than the unique features, their theories aim at. They might also argue that the case-study approach, in which violent conflicts are studied one by one and which permits the telling of nuanced and complicated stories, suffers from the fundamental flaw of lacking interest in absent effects and controls – namely, in that which explains what really distinguishes these cases of violent conflict from cases where such conflicts do not occur.

PART 2
Empirical explorations

What follows is an attempt to shed additional empirical light on some of the assumptions and mechanisms involved in the stories referred to above. Use will be made of the Afrobarometer opinion survey. The text is exploratory and should be seen as identifying future research directions rather than as final evidence. It also serves to illustrate the potential value of this kind of survey data in relation to these themes. The following questions will be posed in respect of the data:
- Do group grievances combine with horizontal inequalities?
- Do political and economic grievances come together?
- How do horizontal vs. vertical inequality indicators perform when correlated with grievance and conflict indicators?
- How do horizontal inequalities and group grievances evolve over time in a conflict setting (as illustrated by the Kenya case)?

To avoid misunderstanding from the start, it should be noted that no claims of causality or directions of causality will be made in these explorations. The approach is, rather, descriptive, but does, of course, lend itself to the formulation or questioning of hypotheses, which may involve assumptions about causal directions.

Data sources
Use will be made of survey data from the fourth round of the Afrobarometer. This survey is repeated every three or four years, and currently covers 20 countries in sub-Saharan Africa (see Table 1 for coverage). The coverage is expanding, with the next round of surveys expected to increase the number of countries to 25. Sample sizes are in most cases 1,200 interviewed persons per country (a few countries have sample sizes of above 2,000). There are some disadvantages to this database (limited number of countries and sample sizes not ideal for disaggregation), but also some unique advantages for our purposes here: it permits connections to be made, on the one hand, between social and economic factors and, on the other, between perceptions and attitudes in relation to identities. In theory, it is also a survey that should be able to measure change over time, including how people may move in and out of identities and attach different degrees of salience to them.

The barometer includes a comprehensive set of questions referring to socio-economic background variables as well as identity-related factors such as religion, region, language and ethnic group. In principle, it is possible to break down indicators per identity group, although sample sizes put a limit on how accurate such indicators are for smaller groups. When it comes to ethnic identity,

Table 1. Afrobarometer round 4 countries, registered conflicts and level of domestic armed conflict

Afro-barometer Country, round 4 (2008)	War and minor conflict since 2000 (UCDP 2010)	Non-state conflict/ One-sided conflicts since 2000 (UCDP 2010)	Level of domestic armed conflict (EIU/ Mo Ibrahim 2010)
Nigeria	Niger Delta 2003	Niger Delta + various other	25
Uganda	Northern Uganda	Northern Uganda, various	25
Liberia	Civil war 2003		50
Mali	Mali-Azawad 2007–09		50
Senegal	Casamance 2003	Various related to Casamance	50
Ghana		2002 and 2008/North	75
Kenya		Post election conflicts, 2008	75
Madagascar	Political violence 2009	Rajeolina vs Ravalomanana	75
Tanzania		Zanzibar 2001, post-election	75
Zimbabwe	Government-civilians 2008		75
Benin			100
Botswana			100
Burkina Faso			100
Cape Verde			100
Lesotho			100
Malawi			100
Mozambique			100
Namibia			100
South Africa			100

Sources: UCDP database 2010, EIU Mo Ibrahim 2010. See also explanations in text and Annex 1.

respondents are also asked to indicate how much importance they attach to that identity as compared to national identity.

Sample

Table 1 displays the list of countries included, with the second and third columns indicating any conflict registered in the Uppsala Conflict Data Programme (UCDP) database since 2000 (either war/minor conflict or non-state/one-sided conflicts). The fourth column displays the ranking of these countries in terms of the level of domestic armed conflict (an assessment by the Economist Intelligence Unit commissioned by the Mo Ibrahim Foundation).

Main indicators

The ethnic identity question in the survey is exploited to make a breakdown of indicators per ethnic group. Smaller ethnic identity groups (below 5 per cent of the respondents of the national survey, or approximately 60 respondents) are excluded. This still leaves us with 112 ethnic groups. A comprehensive list of these 112 groups is attached as Annex 2. As revealed by this list, what the Afro-barometer has identified as ethnic groups may not be strictly comparable across countries. One could think of "politically more relevant" groupings in many cases. [3] However, we have refrained from any recategorisation into politically more relevant groups, as that would be to adjust the sample beforehand in relation to some of the dimensions we want to explore.

The breakdown into ethnic groups obviously creates large margins of error for the indicator of an individual group, particularly if it is small, but as long as this is "random noise" it is less of a problem when studying the overall pattern. For each one of these ethnic groups, we elaborate the following indicators, where a distinction is made between "group grievance" indicators (i.e., respondent's perceptions of the relative position of his/her group) and "group inequality" indicators (relative position of the group calculated on the basis of characteristics of individuals who have stated that they belong to the group).

Group grievances
- *Economic Discontent*: share of respondents of the ethnic group answering that the group's economic conditions are worse or much worse than other groups in the country.
- *Political Discontent*: share of respondents of the ethnic group answering that the group has less or much less political influence than other groups in the country.
- *Unfair Treatment Discontent*: share of respondents of the ethnic group answering that the group is often or always treated unfairly by the government.

Group inequalities
- *Lived Poverty Index/national average*: The index is based on the proportion of respondents in the group answering that they, or someone in the family, have often or many times gone without a) food, b) clean water, c) medicine or medical treatment, d) fuel to cook food, and e) cash income. The index is

---

3.   For instance, in Cape Verde the question does not seem to have made sense, with most respondents answering "African" or "national identity" or "don't know." Botswana, which is often described as a largely homogeneous society with a shared language, is divided into many small groups, most of which would probably be categorised as a single grouping if in a larger country.

then divided by the national average, so that groups with an indicator above unity are the ones above the national average in terms of lived poverty.[4]

- *Asset Index of the group/national average*: The index is based on the proportion of respondents in the group answering that they own a) a radio, b) a TV, and c) a motor vehicle. The index is then divided by the national average.
- *Political Intimidation Fear/divided by national average*: The indicator is based on the proportion of respondents in the group who answered they often or always fear political intimidation. The indicator is then divided by the national average.

Furthermore, at the national level, the following indicators are elaborated:

Group grievances, national level
- *Economic Discontent, Political Discontent and Unfair Treatment Discontent*: As above, but now as national averages.

Group inequalities, national level
- *Horizontal GINI Lived Poverty Index:* This indicator measures the inequality between ethnic groups in a country in terms of lived poverty, calculated according to the formula (where y=national average Lived Poverty Index, y_r=Lived Poverty Index of group r, p_r=share of population for group r, see Stewart 2008, p. 104):

$$(1/2y) \sum\sum p_r p_s \; |\, y_r - y_s\,|$$

- *Horizontal GINI Asset Index*: Same as above, but based on the Asset Index.
- *Horizontal GINI Bribe Index*: Elaborated in the case of Kenya. The index is based on the proportion of respondents in the (language) group answering that, a few times or often, they have paid a bribe related to a) a permit, b) water and sanitation services, and c) police. A horizontal GINI is then calculated based on the formula above.

A distinction is made between three types of variation that we may explore by using this kind of data: i) variation among groups, ii) cross-country variation in national aggregates, and iii) variation over time.

i) Variation among groups:
   Do group grievances combine with horizontal inequalities?
   And do political and economic grievances come together?

The first question to be approached is the assumed link from externally measured horizontal inequalities between groups to people's perceptions of such in-

4. Ideally, this kind of poverty index should be calculated by use of principal component analysis to give different weights to the different components of the index. To keep things simple, here we just add the components ("1" if you have and "0" if you do not have) and divide by number of components. Getting a "1," full score, then means you have often or many times "gone without" all components (food, clean water, medicine, etc.).

equalities between groups (i.e., the assumed step from group inequality to group grievance discussed above in the Stewart story). The correlations between the two sets of indicators are shown in Table 2.

Table 2 illustrates that "actual" group disadvantages, as measured by these indicators, do tend to translate into perceptions that one's group also is disadvantaged. All correlations have the expected sign. The correlation is strongest between the Lived Poverty Index of the group, as compared to the national average, and perceptions that the economic conditions of one's group are worse/much worse than for other groups (labeled "Economic Discontent"). Lived Poverty Index also correlates rather well with the perception of being politically disadvantaged. However, the correlations are by no means perfect.

Table 2. Correlation matrix between indicators of group inequalities and group grievances

Indicators of group inequalities	Indicators of group grievances		
	Economic Discontent	Political Discontent	Unfair Treatment Discontent
Lived Poverty Index/national average	,329**	,271**	0,154
Asset Index/national average	−,266**	−0,169	−0,129
Political Intimidation Fear/national average	0,085	0,131	0,179

Note: Two-tailed correlations based on 112 ethnic groups.
** = significance at 1 per cent level, * = significance at 5 per cent level
Source: Afrobarometer round 4 (2008)

Diagram 1 reveals the overall pattern between the Lived Poverty Index/national average and the Economic Discontent indicator (reminding the reader that the margins of error are quite large for individual groups). The positions in the diagram of some groups that are well known for having been exposed to conflicts seem to fit the Stewart story very well, but there are clear exceptions. The three Northern Ugandan groups (Acholi, Langi, Ateso) score high on both indicators. Luo, Kalenjin and Kikuyu in Kenya are all better off than the national Lived Poverty average, but score very differently in terms of economic discontent (more on the Kenyan groups below). The same is true of Shona and Ndebele in Zimbabwe. Dogomba in Ghana is a case where the Lived Poverty Index is clearly above the national average, but without being translated into a high score on Economic Discontent.

A potential direction for future research efforts could be to map these mismatches, namely groups that perceive themselves as being economically worse off than other groups, while poverty indicators tell another story. Is it because they are economically disadvantaged in dimensions not covered by these indices? Because the national average is not the relevant point of reference? Or does it simply reflect some measurement error?

Through these indicators we may also explore how well perceived economic and political group disadvantages go hand in hand (recall hypothesis 2 of the Stewart story above, according to which conflict is more likely with consistent horizontal inequalities). Diagram 2 shows a fairly strong correlation in the sense that groups which perceive themselves as being worse off economically also perceive themselves as being less influential politically (R^2=0.735). But there are some striking exceptions, such as the Luo in Kenya (this survey was carried out after post-electoral negotiations brought Odinga to the post as prime minister). The Ndebele in Zimbabwe represent the opposite case, where grievances seem to be more a matter of relative political influence than of relative economic conditions.

Diagram 1. Lived poverty index and economic discontent among 112 ethnic groups

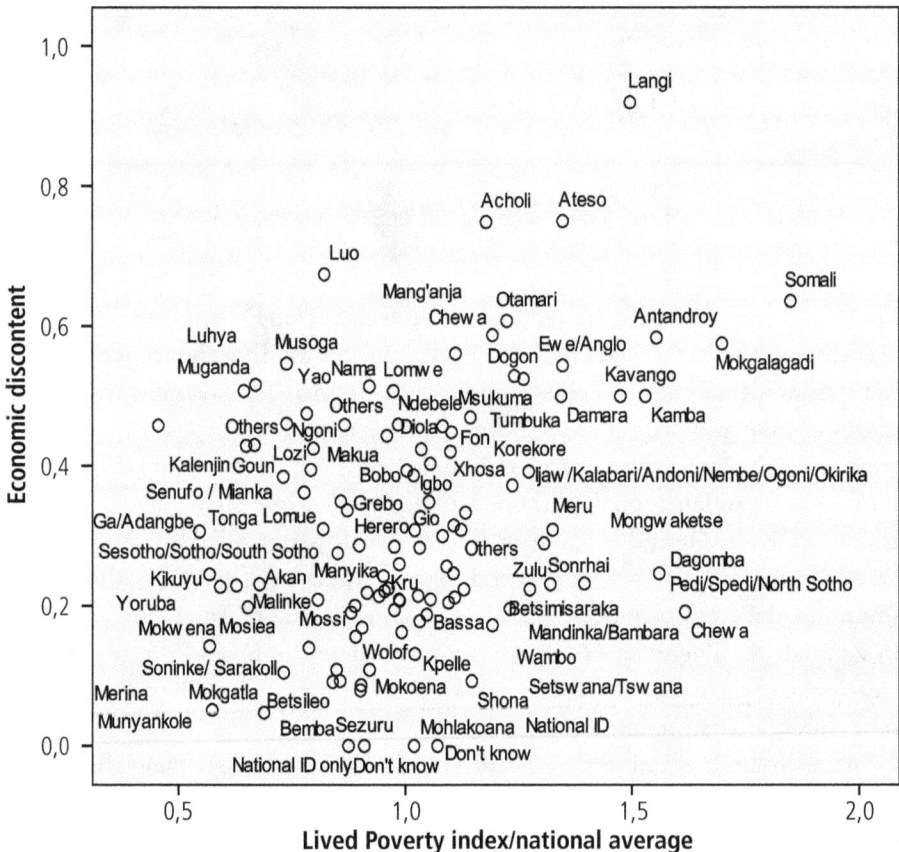

Diagram 2. Economic and political discontent among 112 ethnic groups

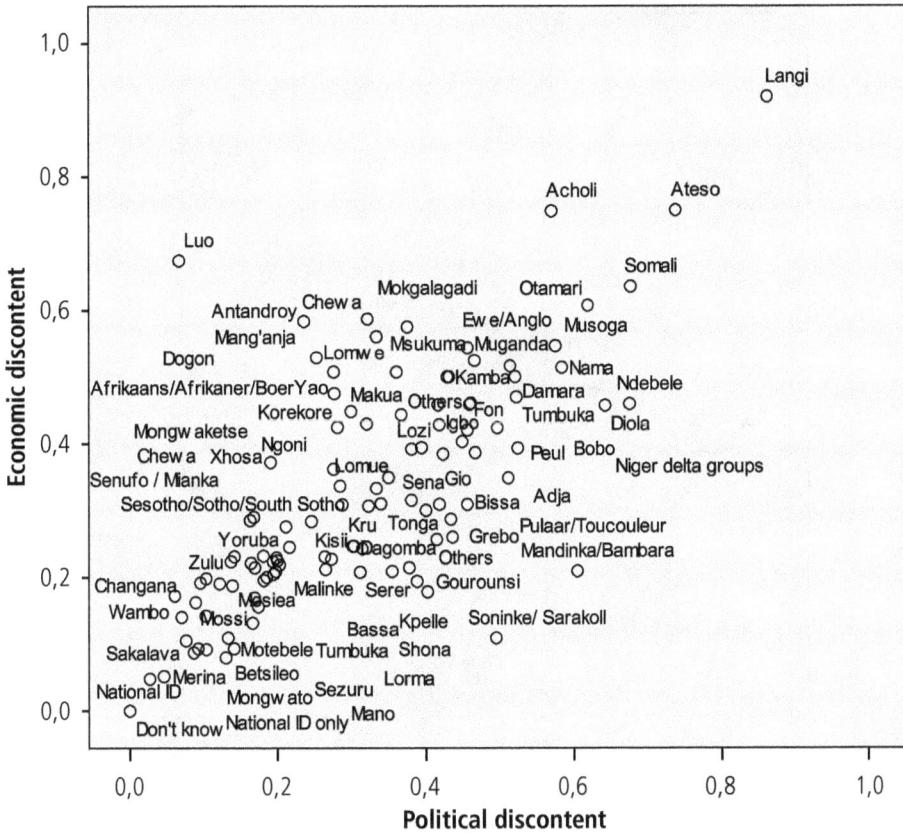

ii) Cross-country variation:
     Horizontal vs. vertical inequality, national level

We now move to the level of indicators at the national level. How do these different horizontal inequalities between ethnic groups in a country correlate with the indicators on grievances and on domestic violent conflict? And how do these horizontal inequalities compare with vertical inequalities as a correlate of indicators on grievances and conflict?

In Diagram 3, the horizontal GINI coefficients for lived poverty are plotted against the vertical GINI coefficients found in international databases (here WIDER and World Bank/WDI, see Annex 1). The vertical GINI was the indicator the Collier story used as a proxy for grievances. As shown, the correlation between horizontal and vertical inequality is there, but the match is not very strong. There are severe problems with data reliability and comparability here, but it seems safe to conclude that horizontal GINIs are likely to tell a different story from vertical GINIs, something that has already been shown in previous studies (Stewart, p. 96).

Diagram 3. Horizontal and vertical GINI

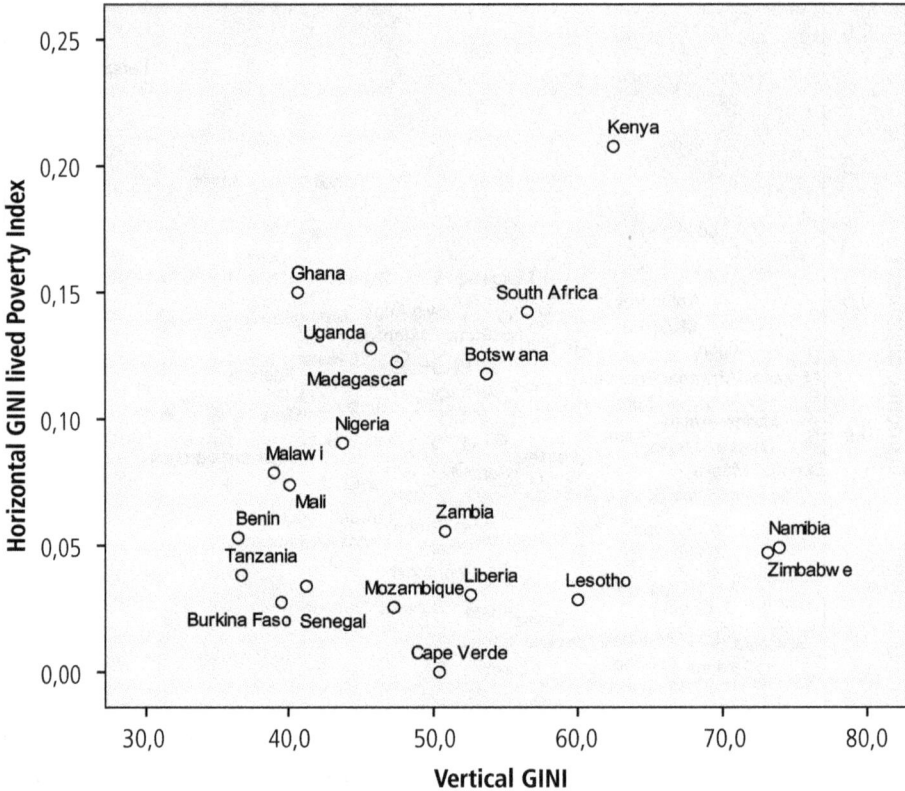

Table 3 compares how the horizontal GINI and the vertical GINI correlate with the different indicators on discontent and the indicator on the level of domestic armed conflict (from EIU/Mo Ibrahim Foundation, see Annex 1). As revealed by the table, the horizontal GINI correlates much more strongly with the indicators on discontent and on domestic armed conflict than is the case for the vertical GINI. No large conclusions will be drawn from a sample of 20 countries, but the table is a strong indication that vertical GINI coefficients are unlikely to perform well as a proxy for grievances. In this sample, the vertical GINI is not even positively correlated with most of the group grievance indicators. (The role of horizontal inequalities in predicting violent conflicts is more convincingly shown, based on larger samples, in Östby 2008 and Cederman *et al.* 2010).

iii) Variation over time:
   Horizontal inequalities and group grievances – the case of Kenya 2002–08

Among the countries included in the Afrobarometer, Kenya is one that recently passed through a violent conflict, with surveys carried out before and right after

Table 3. Horizontal and vertical GINIs correlated with indicators on discontent and conflict

	Horizontal GINI Lived Poverty Index	Horizontal GINI Asset Index	Vertical GINI (income inequality)
Economic Discontent	,423	,239	−,291
Political Discontent	,134	,334	−,292
Unfair Treatment Discontent	,431	,152	,158
Level of Domestic Armed Conflict	−,209	−,005	,210

Note: Two-tailed correlations based on 20 countries.
Sources: Afrobarometer round 4 (2008), Vertical GINI: WIDER and World Bank WDI, latest year available. Level of Domestic Armed Conflict: EIU/Mo Ibrahim Foundation, 2010. See also Annex 1.

the electoral violence in 2008. The 2003 survey was carried out in September, just eight months after the installation of President Kibaki, who had led an electoral "rainbow" coalition against KANU and the Moi regime. When the 2005 survey was carried out in September, it was a few months prior to the constitutional referendum and after the rainbow coalition had fallen apart and Kikuyus were perceived to have taken over the government.[5] The contested election results in 2007 led to widespread violence, which, at least to many outsiders, came unexpectedly. The violence abated with the power-sharing deal between President Kibaki and Prime Minister Odinga. The last Afrobarometer survey was carried out shortly after that deal, in October-November 2008.

The 2008 Kenyan conflict had, as often is the case, many dimensions. Few would, however, deny that political mobilisation around ethnic identities was one of them.

The question to be explored here is how some of the indicators identified above performed during these three years in Kenya. Was the conflict preceded by widening horizontal inequalities, as the Stewart story would predict (see Stewart's hypothesis 3, above)? Did horizontal inequalities go hand in hand with perceptions and grievances? Did ethnic identities become stronger as a result of the conflict, which to some extent is to be expected from the Zartman story's "creed phase"?

Table 4 displays some of the indicators of interest. We may summarise Table 4 as follows:

---

5. See Wrong (2009) for a vivid account of the atmosphere in the country over these years.

Table 4. Kenya 2003–08

	2003	2005	2008
Individual Grievance (nat. average)			
Your economic conditions vs others (worse+much worse)	0,24	0,35	0,50
Ethnic Group Grievance (nat. average)			
Political Discontent	na	0,38	0,37
Economic Discontent	na	0,19	0,32
Poverty and Inequality			
National average, Lived Poverty Index	0,23	0,26	0,19
Ethnic Group GINI, Lived Poverty Index	0,08	0,16	0,21
Bribe paying			
National average, Bribe Index	0,12	0,12	0,09
Ethnic Group GINI, Bribe Index	0,18	0,30	0,24
Strength of Ethnic Identity			
Ethnic ID only or "more than national"	na	0,16	0,12

Note: Data from the Afrobarometer rounds 2, 3 and 4. GINI coefficients calculated using the seven largest language groups in Kenya (approximately 80 per cent of the population). Language groups rather than ethnic groups have been used as the 2003 survey lacked the question on ethnic group (less of a problem in the Kenyan case, where there is a strong overlap between languages and ethnic groups).

- Individual grievances (share of respondents indicating that their economic conditions vs. others were worse or much worse) rose sharply between 2003 and 2008. Also, group grievances in terms of economic discontent rose sharply between 2005 and 2008 (data for 2003 not available).
- Political discontent (national average for respondents considering that their ethnic group had less or much less political influence) remained the same. However, as revealed by Diagram 4, this unchanged aggregate indicator hides a massive turnaround among the major ethnic groups, with some perceiving a loss of political influence, and vice versa.
- The national average for Lived Poverty Index did not change much. In fact, it seems rather to have improved between 2005 and 2008.
- The horizontal GINI for the Lived Poverty Index increased rather sharply. Diagram 5 reveals how the GINI for lived poverty has moved together with the individual perceptions of being "worse off" in terms of economic conditions, while the Lived Poverty Index (national average) has remained more or less unaltered.

- As national average, the Bribe Index has not changed, but there has been a clear change in how the payments of these bribes are distributed between different ethnic groups, with the group GINI for bribe payments increasing. For instance, Luos and Kalenjins sharply increased bribe paying in 2005 and reduced it again in 2008, while the opposite is the case for Kikuyu and Meru/Embu.
- When it comes to strength of ethnic identity (share of respondents with "ethnic ID only" or "more ethnic ID than national") the conflict did not result in more of ethnic identity from 2005 to 2008.
- The table also reveals that already by 2005, two years before the eruption of violence, there were early warning signals: rising horizontal inequalities, sharply increased grievances and discrimination reflected in the ethnic profile of bribe paying.

Diagram 4. Kenya: Ethnic group's political influence vs others
(% answering less+much less)

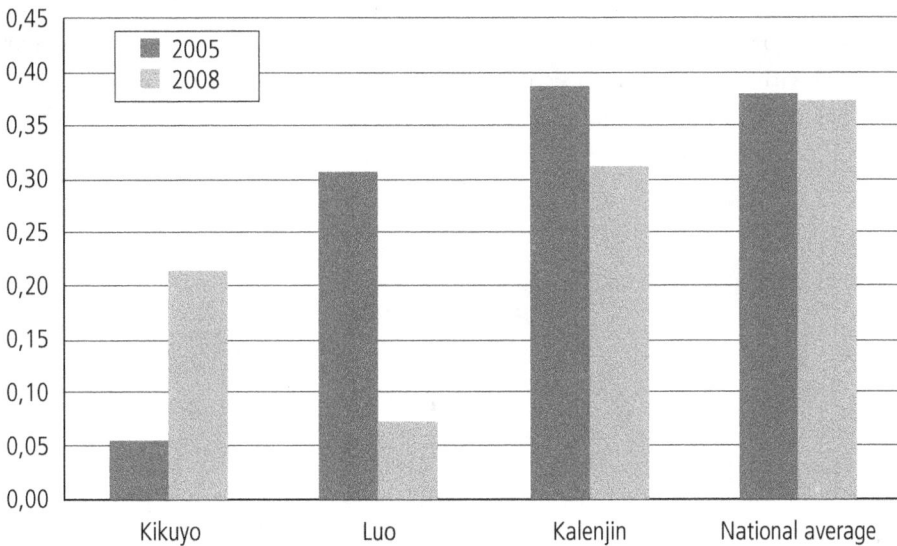

Kenya therefore does appear to fit the Stewart story quite well: horizontal inequalities appear to have widened prior to the conflict, while there are also indications that these changing inequalities are reflected in perceptions and grievances. (Stewart 2008b makes the same point but based on other data sources.) There are also some puzzles here regarding the creed phase of the Zartman story. It does seem as if this conflict, which had undeniably strong ethnic elements in it, combined with a strengthening of the national identity, as measured at the end of 2008. This strengthening of national identity between 2005 and 2008 seems

Diagram 5. Kenya: Horizontal inequality, lived poverty and individual perceptions of relative economic position

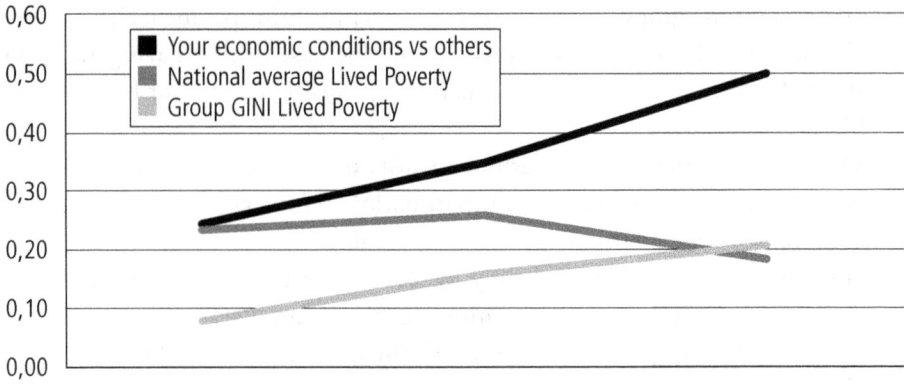

to have occurred in all ethnic groups, and particularly among Luos. Moreover, the more exclusive options in answer to this ethnic vs. national identity question moved accordingly, that is, a lower share answered "ethnic ID only" and an increasing share answered "only national ID." In 2008, just after these violent conflicts with strong ethnic ingredients, only 12 per cent of Kenyans considered their ethnic identity to be more important than their national identity.

Conclusion

The four stories reviewed could be seen as attempts to formulate grand theories about the causes of civil war, that is, to reveal patterns that repeat themselves over time and space. Case-study oriented scholars might question the approach and argue that studies of individual cases will reveal additional complexities and nuances that such grand stories are unable to capture. What additional contributions do these macro-models provide a person trying to make sense of ongoing conflicts in, say, Afghanistan or Eastern Congo? I would defend all four of them in their attempts to paint the large picture (as long as it is not interpreted deterministically, applying always and everywhere). For those involved in formulating more general policies, or in prioritising investments in global public goods, the large picture is relevant. Furthermore, the macro view may also inspire alternative interpretations of case-study findings, and vice versa.

Each of the four stories reviewed carries a favoured set of policy recommendations. Should, for instance, the focus be on reducing the feasibility of financing rebellions (Collier), on addressing horizontal inequalities (Stewart), on reinforcing state capabilities at an early stage of conflict (Zartman) or on restoring citizens' trust in state institutions (World Bank)? The answers to these questions are by no means irrelevant to actors engaged in conflict-prevention and management.

The empirical explorations presented here do not yield any final judgments on the stories. However, it appears that indicators of horizontal inequalities have a larger potential than those for vertical inequality in predicting the level of grievance and possibly also the risk of civil war. Horizontal inequality is not captured in the empirical applications of the Collier-Hoeffler model, where only vertical inequality is used as a proxy for grievances. The downplaying of the role of factors related to grievances in the Collier story may thus be premature.

The explorations in this paper have been able to identify correlations, but without establishing causal relations. Relative disadvantage and grievance may cause a conflict as well as be caused by it, and people may move in and out of different identities as a by-product of conflict and a group's disadvantages. It is difficult to imagine how causal directions can be approached without access to more time-series data. Such data is, however, to be expected when future surveys deliver their results.

Finally, there are a number of issues that could, with additional time and effort, be explored:

- Inequality indicators could be elaborated across more identities (region, religion, language, all available in the Afrobarometer) and more dimensions (access to education, health services and more indicators on political influence and participation). A picture of overlaps and diversity of inequality across identities and dimensions, and the links to grievances, could hence be created. This could also shed additional light on some of the puzzles revealed in the diagrams above (for instance, strong economic group grievances not matched by indicators on relative position regarding poverty and assets).

- Trust indicators – available in various dimensions in the Afrobarometer – have still not been explored. These indicators could shed more light on the perspectives presented in World Development Report 2011.

- The Afrobarometer, the Latinobarometer and the Asiabarometer have pooled their common questions into what has been labelled the Global Barometer.[6] The number of common questions in these surveys is limited, but for certain aspects it should be possible to extend analysis to a global sample.

- Not attempted in this paper is a move to the level of the individual using micro-econometric tools over a sample of some 25,000 respondents. This would enable group characteristics in terms of inequality to be studied as a predictor of individual attitudes.

---

6. Total 53 countries, available at http://www.globalbarometer.net/

References

Acemoglu D. and J. Robinson, 2006, *Economic Origins of Dictatorship and Democracy.* New York: Cambridge University Press.

Akerlof G. and R. Kranton, 2000, "Economics and Identity", *Quarterly Journal of Economics* 115 (3).

Akerlof G. and R. Kranton, 2010, *Identity Economics.* Princeton University Press.

Arnson C. and W. Zartman (eds), 2005, *Rethinking the Economics of War, The Intersection of Need, Creed and Greed.* Washington: Woodrow Wilson Center Press.

Bircan C., T. Bruck and M. Vothknecht, 2010, *Violent conflict and inequality.* Working Paper 129, Brooks World Poverty Institute.

Brown G. and A. Langer, 2010, *Conceptualizing and Measuring Ethnicity.* JICA-RI Working Paper 9, JICA Research Institute.

—, 2011, "Horizontal inequalities and conflict: A critical review and research agenda", *Conflict Security and Development* 10 (1), March.

Brubaker R., 2002, "Ethnicity without groups", *European Journal of Sociology* XLIII (2).

Cederman L., N. Weidmann and K. Gleditsch, 2010, *Horizontal Inequalities and Ethno-Nationalist Civil War: A Global Comparison.* Working paper presented at the Annual Meeting of the American Political Science Association, 2–5 September 2010.

Collier P. and A. Hoeffler, 1998, "On the economic causes of civil war", *Oxford Economic Papers* 50.

—, 2002, "On the Incidence of Civil War in Africa", *Journal of Conflict Resolution* 46 (1).

—, 2004, "Greed and grievance in civil war", *Oxford Economic Papers* 56.

Collier P., A. Hoeffler and D. Rohner, 2008, *Beyond Greed and Grievance: Feasibility of Civil War,* Department of Economics, University of Oxford.

Collier P., A. Hoeffler and M. Söderbom, 2004, "On the duration of civil war", *Journal of Peace Research* 41:253.

Collier P. and N. Sambanis, 2005, *Understanding Civil War.* World Bank 2005.

Esteban J. and D. Ray, 1994, "On the measurement of polarization", *Econometrica* 62.

—, 2011, "Linking conflict to inequality and polarization", *American Economic Review,* 101:4.

Fearon J. and D. Laitin, 2003, "Ethnicity, insurgency and civil war", *American Political Science Review* 97 (1).

Grossman, H., 1991, "A general equilibrium model of insurrections", *American Economic Review* 81 (4).

Mancini L., 2008, "Horizontal Inequality and Communal Violence: Evidence from Indonesian Districts", in F. Stewart (ed.), *Horizontal Inequality and Conflic.* New York: Palgrave.

Murshed S.M. and S. Gates, 2005, "Spatial Horizontal Inequalities and the Maoist Insurgency in Nepal", *Review of Development Economics* 9 (1).

North D., J. Wallis and B. Weingast, 2009, *Violence and Social Orders – A Conceptual Framework for Interpreting Recorded Human Histor.* New York: Cambridge University Press.

Kalyvas S., 2003, "The ontology of 'political violence': action and identity in civil wars", *Perspectives on Politics* 1 (3), September.

—, 2007, "Civil Wars" in C. Boix and S. Stokes (eds), *The Oxford Handbook of Comparative Politics.* Oxford: Oxford University Press.

Langer A. and U. Ukiwo, 2008, "Ethnicity, Religion and the State in Ghana and Nigeria: Perceptions from the Street", in F Stewart (ed.), *Horizontal Inequality and Conflict:* New York: Palgrave.

Östby, G., 2008, "Inequalities, the political environment and civil conflict: Evidence from 55 developing countries" in F. Stewart (ed.), *Horizontal Inequality and Conflict.* New York: Palgrave.

Stewart F. (ed.), 2008, *Horizontal Inequality and Conflict.* New York: Palgrave.

—, 2008b, *Note for Discussion: Kenya, Horizontal Inequalities and the Political Disturbances of 2008.* CRISE, downloaded at: http://www.crise.ox.ac.uk/copy/kenya_note.pdf

World Bank, 2011, *World Development Report – Conflict, Security and Development.* World Bank.

Wrong M., 2009, *It's Our Turn to Eat, the Story of a Kenyan Whistle Blower.* London: HarperCollins.

Annex 1: Data

Afrobarometer indicators

Elaborated from Afrobarometer round 4 (2008). The Kenya case also makes use of the Afrobarometers round 2 and 4 (2002 and 2005). Data and questionnaires available for download at: http://www.afrobarometer.org/

Breakdowns made according to ethnic group of respondents (language groups in the Kenya case). Groups smaller than 5 per cent of country sample not included. List of ethnic groups per country available as Annex 2.

For explanations on elaborations of data, see relevant sections of the text.

Level of Domestic Violence

Indicator based on assessment made by the Economist Intelligence Unit and commissioned by Mo Ibrahim Foundation (2010), available for download at: http://www.moibrahimfoundation.org/en/section/the-ibrahim-index

Vertical Gini

From WIDER's data set on income inequality, downloaded at http://www.wider.unu.edu/research/Database/en_GB/database/

(Cape Verde and Liberia from World Bank/WDI)

Violent conflicts (Table 1)

From Uppsala UCDP database, downloaded at: http://www.pcr.uu.se/research/UCDP/

Annex 2: Countries in Afrobarometer round 4 and ethnic groups
(population share > 5 per cent)

Country	Ethnic group	Country	Ethnic group
Benin	Fon	Lesotho	Motaung
Benin	Adja	Lesotho	Mosiea
Benin	Yoruba	Liberia	Kpelle
Benin	Bariba	Liberia	Bassa
Benin	Otamari	Liberia	Grebo
Benin	Goun	Liberia	Mano
Botswana	Mokalanga	Liberia	Lorma
Botswana	Mongwato	Liberia	Gio
Botswana	Mongwaketse	Liberia	Kru
Botswana	Mokwena	Madagascar	Merina
Botswana	Mokgatla	Madagascar	Betsileo
Botswana	Mokgalagadi	Madagascar	Betsimisaraka
Botswana	Motswapong	Madagascar	Antandroy
Burkina Faso	Mossi	Madagascar	Sakalava
Burkina Faso	Peul	Malawi	Chewa
Burkina Faso	Bissa	Malawi	Lomwe
Burkina Faso	Gourounsi	Malawi	Ngoni
Burkina Faso	Bobo	Malawi	Yao
Cape Verde	National ID	Malawi	Tumbuka
Cape Verde	African	Malawi	Mang'anja
Cape Verde	Don't know	Mali	Bambara
Ghana	Akan	Mali	Peulh/Fulfulde
Ghana	Ewe/Anglo	Mali	Senufo /Mianka
Ghana	Ga/Adangbe	Mali	Soninke/Sarakoll
Ghana	Dagomba	Mali	Malinke
Ghana	Others	Mali	Sonrhai
Kenya	Kikuyu	Mali	Dogon
Kenya	Luhya	Mozambique	Makua
Kenya	Luo	Mozambique	Don't know
Kenya	Kalenjin	Mozambique	Changana
Kenya	Kamba	Mozambique	Lomue
Kenya	Somali	Mozambique	Sena
Kenya	Kisii	Namibia	Wambo
Kenya	Meru	Namibia	Kavango
Lesotho	Mofokeng	Namibia	Damara
Lesotho	Motebele	Namibia	Herero
Lesotho	Mokoena	Namibia	Nama
Lesotho	Mohlakoana	Nigeria	Hausa

Country	Ethnic group
Nigeria	Yoruba
Nigeria	Igbo
Nigeria	Ijaw/Kalabari/Andoni/Nembe/Ogoni/Okirika
Nigeria	Others
Senegal	Wolof
Senegal	Pulaar/Toucouleur
Senegal	Serer
Senegal	Mandinka/Bambara
Senegal	Diola
South Africa	Zulu
South Africa	Afrikaans/Afrikaner/Boer
South Africa	Xhosa
South Africa	National ID only
South Africa	Setswana/Tswana
South Africa	Coloured
South Africa	Sesotho/Sotho/South Sotho
South Africa	Pedi/Spedi/North Sotho
Tanzania	Msukuma
Tanzania	Others
Uganda	Muganda
Uganda	Munyankole
Uganda	Musoga
Uganda	Langi
Uganda	Acholi
Uganda	Ateso
Zambia	Bemba
Zambia	Tonga
Zambia	Lozi
Zambia	Chewa
Zambia	Tumbuka
Zimbabwe	Shona
Zimbabwe	Sezuru
Zimbabwe	Ndebele
Zimbabwe	Karanga
Zimbabwe	Korekore
Zimbabwe	Manyika

DISCUSSION PAPERS PUBLISHED BY THE INSTITUTE

Recent issues in the series are available electronically for download free of charge
www.nai.uu.se

1. Kenneth Hermele and Bertil Odén, *Sanctions and Dilemmas. Some Implications of Economic Sanctions against South Africa.* 1988. 43 pp. ISBN 91-7106-286-6

2. Elling Njål Tjönneland, *Pax Pretoriana. The Fall of Apartheid and the Politics of Regional Destabilisation.* 1989. 31 pp. ISBN 91-7106-292-0

3. Hans Gustafsson, Bertil Odén and Andreas Tegen, *South African Minerals. An Analysis of Western Dependence.* 1990. 47 pp. ISBN 91-7106-307-2

4. Bertil Egerö, *South African Bantustans. From Dumping Grounds to Battlefronts.* 1991. 46 pp. ISBN 91-7106-315-3

5. Carlos Lopes, *Enough is Enough! For an Alternative Diagnosis of the African Crisis.* 1994. 38 pp. ISBN 91-7106-347-1

6. Annika Dahlberg, *Contesting Views and Changing Paradigms.* 1994. 59 pp. ISBN 91-7106-357-9

7. Bertil Odén, *Southern African Futures. Critical Factors for Regional Development in Southern Africa.* 1996. 35 pp. ISBN 91-7106-392-7

8. Colin Leys and Mahmood Mamdani, *Crisis and Reconstruction – African Perspectives.* 1997. 26 pp. ISBN 91-7106-417-6

9. Gudrun Dahl, *Responsibility and Partnership in Swedish Aid Discourse.* 2001. 30 pp. ISBN 91-7106-473-7

10. Henning Melber and Christopher Saunders, *Transition in Southern Africa – Comparative Aspects.* 2001. 28 pp. ISBN 91-7106-480-X

11. *Regionalism and Regional Integration in Africa.* 2001. 74 pp. ISBN 91-7106-484-2

12. Souleymane Bachir Diagne, et al., *Identity and Beyond: Rethinking Africanity.* 2001. 33 pp. ISBN 91-7106-487-7

13. Georges Nzongola-Ntalaja, et al., *Africa in the New Millennium.* Edited by Raymond Suttner. 2001. 53 pp. ISBN 91-7106-488-5

14. *Zimbabwe's Presidential Elections 2002.* Edited by Henning Melber. 2002. 88 pp. ISBN 91-7106-490-7

15. Birgit Brock-Utne, *Language, Education and Democracy in Africa.* 2002. 47 pp. ISBN 91-7106-491-5

16. Henning Melber et al., *The New Partnership for Africa's development (NEPAD).* 2002. 36 pp. ISBN 91-7106-492-3

17. Juma Okuku, *Ethnicity, State Power and the Democratisation Process in Uganda.* 2002. 42 pp. ISBN 91-7106-493-1

18. Yul Derek Davids, et al., *Measuring Democracy and Human Rights in Southern Africa.* Compiled by Henning Melber. 2002. 50 pp. ISBN 91-7106-497-4

19. Michael Neocosmos, Raymond Suttner and Ian Taylor, *Political Cultures in Democratic South Africa.* Compiled by Henning Melber. 2002. 52 pp. ISBN 91-7106-498-2

20. Martin Legassick, *Armed Struggle and Democracy. The Case of South Africa.* 2002. 53 pp. ISBN 91-7106-504-0

21. Reinhart Kössler, Henning Melber and Per Strand, *Development from Below. A Namibian Case Study.* 2003. 32 pp. ISBN 91-7106-507-5

22. Fred Hendricks, *Fault-Lines in South African Democracy. Continuing Crises of Inequality and Injustice.* 2003. 32 pp. ISBN 91-7106-508-3

23. Kenneth Good, *Bushmen and Diamonds. (Un) Civil Society in Botswana.* 2003. 39 pp. ISBN 91-7106-520-2

24. Robert Kappel, Andreas Mehler, Henning Melber and Anders Danielson, *Structural Stability in an African Context.* 2003. 55 pp. ISBN 91-7106-521-0

25. Patrick Bond, *South Africa and Global Apartheid. Continental and International Policies and Politics.* 2004. 45 pp. ISBN 91-7106-523-7

26. Bonnie Campbell (ed.), *Regulating Mining in Africa. For whose benefit?* 2004. 89 pp. ISBN 91-7106-527-X

27. Suzanne Dansereau and Mario Zamponi, *Zimbabwe – The Political Economy of Decline.* Compiled by Henning Melber. 2005. 43 pp. ISBN 91-7106-541-5

28. Lars Buur and Helene Maria Kyed, *State Recogni-tion of Traditional Authority in Mozambique. The nexus of Community Representation and State Assist-ance.* 2005. 30 pp. ISBN 91-7106-547-4

29. Hans Eriksson and Björn Hagströmer, *Chad – Towards Democratisation or Petro-Dictatorship?* 2005. 82 pp.ISBN 91-7106-549-

30. Mai Palmberg and Ranka Primorac (eds), *Skinning the Skunk – Facing Zimbabwean Futures.* 2005. 40 pp. ISBN 91-7106-552-0

31. Michael Brüntrup, Henning Melber and Ian Taylor, *Africa, Regional Cooperation and the World Market – Socio-Economic Strategies in Times of Global Trade Regimes.* Com-piled by Henning Melber. 2006. 70 pp. ISBN 91-7106-559-8

32. Fibian Kavulani Lukalo, *Extended Handshake or Wrestling Match? – Youth and Urban Culture Celebrating Politics in Kenya.* 2006.58 pp. ISBN 91-7106-567-9

33. Tekeste Negash, *Education in Ethiopia: From Crisis to the Brink of Collapse.* 2006. 55 pp. ISBN 91-7106-576-8

34. Fredrik Söderbaum and Ian Taylor (eds) *Micro-Regionalism in West Africa. Evidence from Two Case Studies.* 2006. 32 pp. ISBN 91-7106-584-9

35. Henning Melber (ed.), *On Africa – Scholars and African Studies.* 2006. 68 pp. ISBN 978-91-7106-585-8

36. Amadu Sesay, *Does One Size Fit All? The Sierra Leone Truth and Reconciliation Commission Revisited.* 2007. 56 pp. ISBN 978-91-7106-586-5

37. Karolina Hulterström, Amin Y. Kamete and Henning Melber, *Political Opposition in African Countries – The Case of Kenya, Namibia, Zambia and Zimbabwe.* 2007. 86 pp. ISBN 978-7106-587-2

38. Henning Melber (ed.), *Governance and State Delivery in Southern Africa. Examples from Botswana, Namibia and Zimbabwe.* 2007. 65 pp. ISBN 978-91-7106-587-2

39. Cyril Obi (ed.), *Perspectives on Côte d'Ivoire: Between Political Breakdown and Post-Conflict Peace.* 2007. 66 pp. ISBN 978-91-7106-606-6

40. Anna Chitando, *Imagining a Peaceful Society. A Vision of Children's Literature in a Post-Conflict Zimbabwe.* 2008. 26 pp. ISBN 978-91-7106-623-7

41. Olawale Ismail, *The Dynamics of Post-Conflict Reconstruction and Peace Building in West Africa. Between Change and Stability.* 2009.52 pp. ISBN 978-91-7106-637-4

42. Ron Sandrey and Hannah Edinger, *Examining the South Africa–China Agricultural Relationship.* 2009. 58 pp. ISBN 978-91-7106-643-5

43. Xuan Gao, *The Proliferation of Anti-Dumping and Poor Governance in Emerging Economies.* 2009. 41 pp. ISBN 978-91-7106-644-2

44. Lawal Mohammed Marafa, *Africa's Business and Development Relationship with China. Seeking Moral and Capital Values of the Last Economic Frontier.* 2009. xx pp. ISBN 978-91-7106-645-9

45. Mwangi wa Githinji, *Is That a Dragon or an Elephant on Your Ladder? The Potential Impact of China and India on Export Led Growth in African Countries.* 2009. 40 pp. ISBN 978-91-7106-646-6

46. Jo-Ansie van Wyk, *Cadres, Capitalists, Elites and Coalitions. The ANC, Business and Development in South Africa.* 2009. 61 pp. ISBN 978-91-7106-656-5

47. Elias Courson, *Movement for the Emancipation of the Niger Delta (MEND). Political Marginalization, Repression and Petro-Insurgency in the Niger Delta.*2009. 30 pp. ISBN 978-91-7106-657-2

48. Babatunde Ahonsi, *Gender Violence and HIV/AIDS in Post-Conflict West Africa. Issues and Responses.* 2010. 38 pp. ISBN 978-91-7106-665-7

49. Usman Tar and Abba Gana Shettima, *Endangered Democracy? The Struggle over Secularism and its Implications for Politics and Democracy in Nigeria.* 2010. 21 pp. ISBN 978-91-7106-666-4

50. Garth Andrew Myers, *Seven Themes in African Urban Dynamics.*2010. 28 pp. ISBN 978-91-7106-677-0

51. Abdoumaliq Simone, *The Social Infrastructures of City Life in Contemporary Africa.* 2010. 33 pp. ISBN 978-91-7106-678-7

52. Li Anshan, *Chinese Medical Cooperation in Africa. With Special Emphasis on the Medical Teams and Anti-Malaria Campaign.* 2011. 24 pp. ISBN 978-91-7106-683-1

53. Folashade Hunsu, *Zangbeto: Navigating the Spaces Between Oral art, Communal Security And Conflict Mediation in Badagry, Nigeria.* 2011. 27 pp. ISBN 978-91-7106-688-6

54. Jeremiah O. Arowosegbe, *Reflections on the Challenge of Reconstructing Post-Conflict States in West Africa: Insights from Claude Ake's Political Writings*.
2011. 40 pp. ISBN 978-91-7106-689-3

55. Bertil Odén, *The Africa Policies of Nordic Countries and the Erosion of the Nordic Aid Model: A comparative study*.
2011. 66 pp. ISBN 978-91-7106-691-6

56. Angela Meyer, P*eace and Security Cooperation in Central Africa: Developments, Challenges and Prospects*.
2011. 47 pp ISBN 978-91-7106-693-0

57. Godwin R. Murunga, *Spontaneous or Premeditated? Post-Election Violence in Kenya*.
2011. 58 pp. ISBN 978-91-7106-694-7

58. David Sebudubudu & Patrick Molutsi, *The Elite as a Critical Factor in National Development: The Case of Botswana*.
2011. 48 pp. ISBN 978-91-7106-695-4

59. Sabelo J. Ndlovu-Gatsheni, *The Zimbabwean Nation-State Project. A Historical Diagnosis of Identity and Power-Based Conflicts in a Postcolonial State*.
2011. 97 pp. ISBN 978-91-7106-696-1

60. Jide Okeke, *Why Humanitarian Aid in Darfur is not a Practice of the 'Responsibility to Protect'*.
2011. 45 pp. ISBN 978-91-7106-697-8

61. Florence Odora Adong, *Recovery and Development Politics. Options for Sustainable Peacebuilding in Northern Uganda*.
2011, 72 pp. ISBN 978-91-7106-698-5

62. Osita A. Agbu, *Ethnicity and Democratisation in Africa. Challenges for Politics and Development*.
2011, 30 pp. ISBN 978-91-7106-699-2

63. Cheryl Hendricks, *Gender and Security in Africa. An Overview*.
2011, 32 pp. ISBN 978-91-7106-700-5

64. Adebayo O. Olukoshi, *Democratic Governance and Accountability in Africa. In Search of a Workable Framework*.
2011, 25 pp. ISBN 978-91-7106-701-2

65. Christian Lund, *Land Rights and Citizenship in Africa*.
2011, 31 pp. ISBN 978-91-7106-705-0

66. Lars Rudebeck, *Electoral Democratisation in Post-Civil War Guinea-Bissau 1999–2008*.
2011, 31 pp. ISBN 978-91-7106-706-7

67. Kidane Mengisteab, *Critical Factors in the Horn of Africa's Raging Conflicts*.
2011, 39 pp. ISBN 978-91-7106-707-4

68. Solomon T. Ebobrah, *Reconceptualising Democratic Local Governance in the Niger Delta*.
2011, 32 pp. ISBN 978-91-7106-709-8

69. Linda Darkwa, *The Challenge of Sub-regional Security in West Africa. The Case of the 2006 Ecowas Convention on Small Arms and Light Weapons*.
2011, 39 pp. ISBN 978-91-7106-710-4

70. J.Shola Omotola, *Unconstitutional Changes of Government in Africa. What Implications for Democratic Consolidation?*
2011, 49 pp. ISBN 978-91-7106-711-4

71. Wale Adebanwi, *Globally Oriented Citizenship and International Voluntary Service. Interrogating Nigeria's Technical Aid Corps Scheme*.
2011, 81 pp. ISBN 978-91-7106-713-5

72. Göran Holmqvist, *Inequality and Identity. Causes of War?*
2012, 42 pp. ISBN 978-91-7106-714-2

www.ingramcontent.com/pod-product-compliance
Lightning Source LLC
Chambersburg PA
CBHW080209300326
41934CB00039B/3434